D1059684

FOUR LONDON ARCHITECTS 1985-88
Chipperfield Mather Parry Stanton Williams

9H Gallery
London, England
MIT Press
Cambridge, Massachusetts

9H GALLERY
26-28 Cramer Street
London W1M 3HE
Tel: 01 486 3555

This catalogue has been published to coincide with the exhibition 'Four London Architects' held at the 9H Gallery in London, from 16 October to 15 November 1987.

Published by The MIT Press, Cambridge, Massachusetts, 1987

ISBN 0-262-51043-X

9H Gallery would like to thank The Architects' Journal for their generous contribution to the exhibition.

Printed in England by EG Bond Ltd, October 1987

Exhibition coordinated by Diana Periton

Catalogue edited and designed by Richard Burdett and Mika Hadidian

Contents

Passing the flame

Colin Amery

Whenever a few architects are gathered together there should be a discourse. When four young, but not inexperienced, architects are gathered together in London towards the end of the 1980s the discourse has to be intricate, mannered and cautious – reflecting the intriguing transitional phase through which architecture is passing.

It is not insignificant that the gathering of architects happens in London. The city is currently a boom town for British and foreign architects. Recently an American architect of the old school was heard to say that staying in the Savoy Hotel in 1987 was like staying in the Tehran Hilton in the early 1970s. The town is full of visiting developers and entrepreneurs, celebrating the commercialization of the liberal state. The increasing workload forces young designers to examine the exigencies of contemporary practice. Partnerships form and break with the ease of the modern divorce laws. Loyalties are stretched and sometimes broken but somewhere always hovering over the struggling architect are the powerful ghosts of the recent past.

It has been fashionable among some critics and architects to feel that the Modern Movement is over. In its stead there has been a flood of experiments and trials. But the pure doctrine of functionalism lives on and has benefitted from the process of refinement that extravagant investigation of alternatives has brought about. The use of stylistic elements borrowed from the past, usually as a not very confident series of quotations, has made up what we think of as 'post-modernism'. It has been a passing phase – a useful moment to reconsider some of the reasons for the barrenness and unpopularity of so much modern art and architecture. Underlying the work of all four of the practices described in this catalogue and exhibition is an awareness, at varying levels, of the architectural debate of our times. These four firms have not confined their debate and worry to words or the drawing board, but by pursuing the act of building they have been able to make serious interven-

tions that can be judged as concrete signs of the new transitional architecture. Practising architecture is a powerful way of writing a cultural language that consolidates a place in history for our own time. The value of looking at the work of important younger practitioners relatively early in their careers is that it is sometimes possible to see new elements of the architectural language as they form.

What do these designers have in common? They are all competent technicians of their craft. This familiarity with the world of high-tech (Alan Stanton worked with Richard Rogers on the Centre Georges Pompidou and David Chipperfield worked with Norman Foster particularly on the unexecuted BBC London project) forms a background skill that is evident but not violently celebrated. Technology is not for any of the quartet something to be seen as the *deus ex machina* of the modern age. That sort of view of technology which has led to the giantism of some elements of, for example, the Lloyds Building and the Pompidou Centre, is not for them.

What is fascinating about the state of the art of architecture today is that the apparent void in the architectural order is not being filled by technology, but by more traditional values – materials, form, craftsmanship, colour and in a few cases, the implied search for spiritual meanings and contextual reference. It could be argued that the somewhat conservative nature of the work that is illustrated here reflects a respect for tradition that parallels the current British development of popular capitalism, and the apparent return to safe political and artistic values. But this is a conservatism that is also an inventive response to the recent past. The spirit of architects like Carlo Scarpa, Louis Kahn, Terragni, Albini, Loos, infuses much of this work.

All four practices owe a great debt to Le Corbusier and it is an interesting aspect of their work that deserves particular attention. All architects of their generation have been engaged in an important critical re-evaluation of Le Corbusier – and the result has been a

new concentration of his formal qualities and an adaptation of some of his shapes to new materials. At the same time as these plastic qualities of Le Corbusier are being reinterpreted there is considerable interest in the formality and organization, if not the imagery, of the Italian rationalists and their modern interpreters.

The critical and academic preoccupations of this group are not dissimilar to the international preoccupations of their contemporaries. Modernism without its elaborate and often wrong headed social programme lies at the heart of this work. The pure flame has been passed to this generation to reinterpret, but it was not passed before it had been forced to leap some post-modern hurdles in a critical obstacle race.

David Chipperfield has found much of the clarity of his work in his inheritance from Norman Foster but also from his clear and unambiguous appreciation of things Japanese. He has an unusual gift of being able to absorb the whole of a cultural ethos (in this case contemporary Japan) and calmly select the essential elements that when reinterpreted create an original synthesis. His *Issey Miyake fashion shop, Sloane Street, London 1985* first makes its presence felt by a giant-sized door, a huge piece of timber reminiscent of a temple entry. Within the shop is much more like a calm shrine – flat planes of solid and simple materials – sycamore wood, Portland stone, marble and glass. There is a sense of Japanese space – brilliantly achieved without resorting to any copying or pastiche. No false orientalism here. In fact Chipperfield learns from the dignified simplicity of the clothes and like them he eschews colour – relying instead on texture, fine materials and simple form. There is at the same time a commercial reason for the use of space and the uncluttered quality of the section – the whole shop is a stage, a cat-walk for the display of fashion and those who wear and promote it. His approach is similar and just as effective at the *Equipment Shop, Rue Etienne Marcel, Paris.* Another

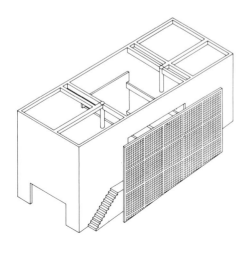

fashionable boutique in a confined narrow space that is made to feel more substantial by solid materials and an ingenious arrangement of levels.

Just as Adolf Loos maximized space and levels in the Muller House and in the Karntner Bar both by use of geometry and rich materials, so these small spaces are enlarged and enhanced. A more recent work by Chipperfield, the conversion of an old London mews building, utilizes many of the same architectural skills but with a broader brush. It is almost like a collage of elements from the modern masters but it also has a quality of illusion about it which combined with the rich palette of materials makes it almost a modern baroque creation. Mies would have liked the use of materials and responded to the marble screen and the quality of the junction details.

Rick Mather is the oldest of this particular quartet and as a result has been able to complete a much more substantial building for a public client. This is a very testing problem in the UK and to have achieved the level of invention and liveliness that he has at the University of East Anglia is a substantial accomplishment. The University building is on another level from his domestic and restaurant designs because of its intricate and at the same time efficient plan. The great reward of the *School of Education/School of Information Studies* at the University of East Anglia is that its apparently quiet and simple exterior conceals a plan of complexity and spaces that are far more intricate than usual in a publicly funded building. The placing in the landscape of Mather's collection of buildings in relation to the giant concrete sculpture by Denys Lasdun certainly provokes questions about the architecture of both the 1960s and the 1980s. The integrity of Lasdun's Corbusian ancestry has a solidity that is almost fundamental as though the buildings are simply added layers of land. Mather delicately places a neatly wrapped and intriguing parcel on the lawn – lighter in weight but full of ideas. No one can miss the Italian rationalist influences on

Mather's circular tower that contains the *Climatic Research Centre* but his placing of this Botta-like tower as a gate to a walk and a walled garden is peculiarly Picturesque and English. Mather's work has a very careful and cool quality that is more conventionally modern although illuminated by a brisk and decisive manipulation of light. It helps to know that Mather's great interest is gardening and his Chinese restaurants with their internal waterfalls, generous planting and reflective white walls have a contemplative garden-like quality that is very rewarding. There are literary parallels in Mather's practice. He has a small opus of polished work that relates to the modern mainstream as Christopher Isherwood does to W.H. Auden. There is something of the hermetic and expensive waiting room about those white restaurants, calm halls for reflecting on the more rational aspects of modernism. They are brave spaces, accomplished essays in a tested language – alternatives and experiments are discouraged because, quite rightly, Mather feels that the gentler interpreters of modernism, like Eileen Gray, have left enough signs for us to follow. There is something solitary about Mather in this group – he is a gentle master of a known style.

Eric Parry's three schemes all reveal him as an architectural romantic. His inspiration is a theoretical view of the recent past and the city combined with a longing for new poetry in architecture. His drawings, particularly the *Villa of the Physicist*, in their actual technique show a tentative majesty that is almost mystical. He has a profound sense of place and architectural language. He would be the first to admit the influence of Dalibor Vesely and Peter Carl, both of them now significant influences on the Cambridge University School of Architecture. They have long propounded a profound respect for tradition as well as promoting an understanding of the contemporary city as a seed bed of ideas for current architects. It is the city and the signs it provides for the continuity of architectural de-

James Stirling and Michael Wilford, History Faculty Building, Cambridge, 1968

Alvaro Siza, bank, Vila do Conde, Portugal, 1985

velopment that roots its innovation in the civic context and the shared memory of the past.

The best example of this approach is the conversion of a Soho premises, *14 Greek Street*, into an animation and graphic studio. Remnants of the past remain in the restored shopfront and the late 17th century staircase – but these are actual solid relics of the past. What Parry has achieved in his extension of the public domain into the almost Pompeian villa entrance hall is a mythic past – a supposed link of a cultural kind that demands associations from the spectator. This small scheme is full of references of this kind – brass trim to the windows are reminiscent of Victorian shopfronts, colours of honey gold and green imply richer materials in the mind's eye than the actual painted plaster. Elements of artifice make the high main hall something of an architectural display. Glass bricks, cut out walls and use of top light draw something elemental from a space that is modestly scaled in reality.

In the artists' studios and in the unbuilt projects there is a sense that a narrative lies behind the architecture. It is narrative that depends for its comprehension upon a somewhat recondite understanding of the collage of modernism. Parry has an intellectual approach to design that demands a parallel understanding from the client – his academicism is likely to bring about fundamental changes in modern architecture if he can match his arguments with craftsmanship and care in execution.

Stanton and Williams grow into architecture together through a complementary interest in exhibition design. Stanton's experience as an architect working on the Pompidou Centre gives him a technological wizardry that can now flower in solid designs with Paul Williams' exhibition work. They aim to combine historical allusion with high powered technical expertise. The fruit of this collaboration in the *Miyake Man Shop* in London is a space of small scale dignity and architectural mood that is powerful beyond its scale. Rich but simple

materials and an almost Escher like staircase rising to a superb Kahnian vault make this an intense and evocative space. Like the work of Chipperfield and Parry, solid materials provide nuances beyond the actual nature of the commission.

The marriage of well tried technical expertise to a more formal and reflective approach to exhibition design is a complementary one. Paul Williams has in the past transformed the notorious and sepulchral Hayward Gallery into an evocative setting for both Rodin and the Romanesque. In the *Royal Academy Gothic Exhibition*, the new partnership has met the challenge of making classical rooms into appropriate settings for medieval objects.

It is not just a skill to deal with lighting, conservation and climate control but also a sense of making 'historical' settings with no element of pastiche. It may be easier to achieve this in the temporary world of exhibition design, but the *Miyake Man* shop demonstrates formal and architectural skills that are timeless and longlasting.

All four practices have inherited the flame of modernism.

All four aim for an architecture that is contextual, solid and uses rich natural materials. Their designs would not have been possible without the work of Foster, Rogers and Stirling and their example of adapting the rules of late 20th century modernism. Without rationalism, high-tech and Stirling's particular narrative historicism the new architecture would not have been possible. Ascetic, spare, austere, calm with elements of a highly informed collage – these are the qualities of this new wave of inspired modern architects.

Their inspiration is the modern movement but they have moved away from the reductionist phase of that style. The discourse has only just begun and looks set to bring about an enriched transformation that is so passionately desired.

Colin Amery is an architectural writer and architectural critic of the *Financial Times*

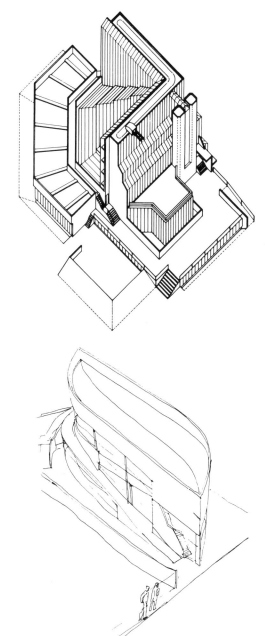

Photograph by Marco di Valdivia

CHIPPERFIELD ASSOCIATES

Issey Miyake Permanente, Sloane Street,
London, 1985
(Armstrong Chipperfield)

Photographs by Peter Cook

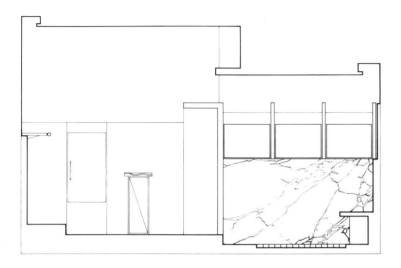

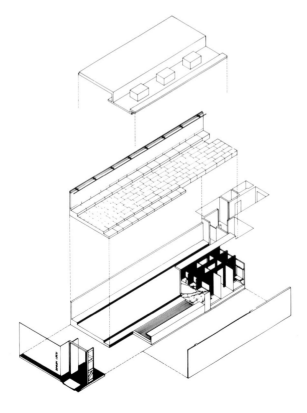

We are engaged in three types of work: new buildings, the conversion of buildings, and the design of small shops, exhibitions and furniture. The particular conditions that have surrounded the evolution of our office – quite different from those of conventional architects' offices – are shared by many others of my generation.

Our approach is influenced by scale: the size of the projects demands that we should control and sometimes develop our formal ideas at a detailed level, so that materials, lighting and construction evolve as an integral part of the design concepts.

Less obviously, our work has to respond in a more precise way to the needs of diverse clients, conditions and programmes. To some degree this defies a stylistic approach and has reinforced our natural tendency to pursue design ideas in two ways: firstly, to form the 'main idea' as a response – to clearly describe and understand the design problem, which in turn suggests how to intervene or operate, the appropriateness of structure, the nature of the existing building, the type of product, the cost, etc. Secondly, more architectural, volumetric and material considerations affect the evolution of the design in, we hope, a non-rhetoric way.

What is apparent in our work within existing buildings is the necessity to be responsive and to interpret the conditions. This process seems to be quite different when confronting new buildings – such as the Museum in Tokyo – where even though one may use one's design experience, the design process itself requires more 'initiative'. The context becomes more personal and less physical, and the object requires 'larger' architectural concepts that transcend detailed design and use of materials.

The shop for Japanese designer Issey Miyake replaced an old shop for the same designer. The old shop resorted to typical Japanese cliches such as black stained timber and 'artistic' pebbles and driftwood. The intention with the design was to avoid such literal cultural references.

Issey Miyake clothes are in themselves a distillation of Japanese tradition, always starting from the material, the clothes are cut out in simple geometric forms. In Miyake's design studio the material inspires form.

The decision then was to adopt a similar approach in the design of the shop. The primary concern was to avoid the fashionable interior and make a good space which should be constructed from simple materials. To this end we looked at the clarity and simplicity of Japanese architecture but tried to avoid borrowing a recognisable language, abstract rather than pictorial, borrowing a spirit rather than a look. The materials are traditional — Portland stone, slate, timber and marble.

The project was carried out by Armstrong Chipperfield in 1985.

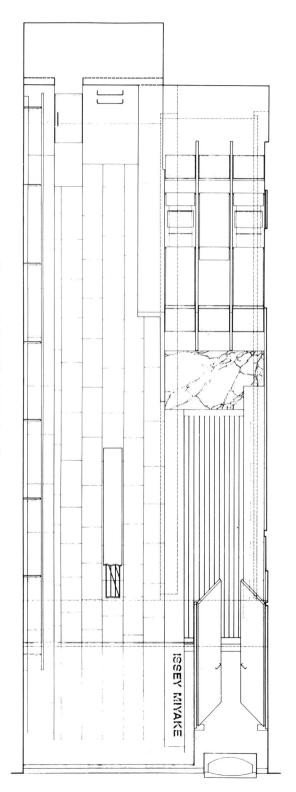

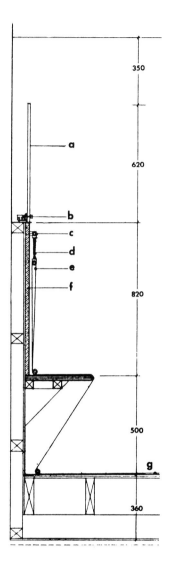

a, sand-blasted glass
b, light fitting
c, stainless-steel fixing
d, tension fitting
e, canvas
f, marble
g, canvas floor

Brownlow Mews, Grays Inn, London, 1987

Brownlow Mews, exterior view

Main staircase lined by the curved elm wall and the grey plaster surface containing a recessed marble handrail

Detailed view of bathroom area

Detailed view of marble handrail
Upper floor plan

Elevational projection from Brownlow Mews
Detailed plan of staircase

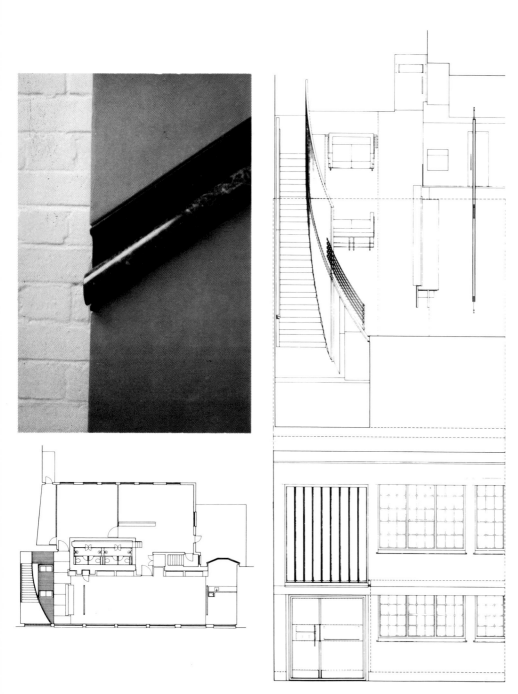

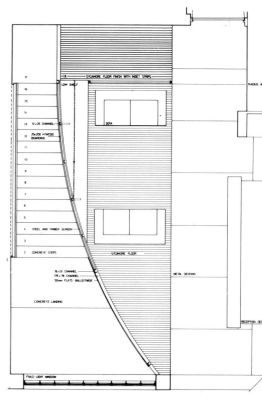

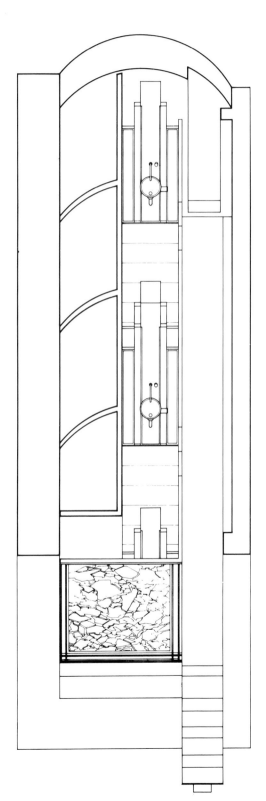

A firm of graphic designers, Carroll, Dempsey and Thirkell, commissioned the practice to provide them with new premises in a recently acquired but run down mews warehouse building near Grays Inn Road, London. The architect acted as main contractor to the job employing joiners and metalworkers as craftsmen in order to concentrate the limited budget on a number of carefully detailed spaces and objects.

As the ground floor was to be sub-let, a staircase entrance to the studios on the first floor was required. The design is accordingly based on a grand staircase between a curved elm and steel wall, and a floating plaster screen with an inset steel and carved marble handrail.

The flooring materials in the reception area at the top of the stairs are stainless steel and narrow sycamore boards with brass insets in the public circulation zone. The reception desk is of painted steel with wood and stainless steel worktops and a black marble face. Simple painted screens enclose the studio space behind the reception, and a new deep storage wall runs the length of the studio.

The WCs in the centre of the building occupy the space of the former ovens, and are reached by steps of folded stainless steel sheet. These areas are enclosed by painted steel frames filled with panels of sandblasted glass, or with mirrors, or, at the entrance, with a sheet of white marble. The wash hand basins are customised salad bowls.

Seibu Department Store, 9th floor, Shibuya,
Tokyo, 1986
View of changing rooms

Apartment, Cleveland Square, London 1985-6
Kitchen and entrance area

Equipment, Rue Etienne Marcel, Paris, 1986

View of steel seat

View from counter

Equipment, Rue Etienne Marcel, Paris,
exploded axonometric

Baker House, Boston, USA, 1986

Private museum, Tokyo, 1987

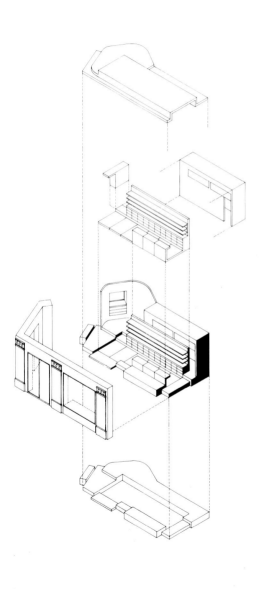

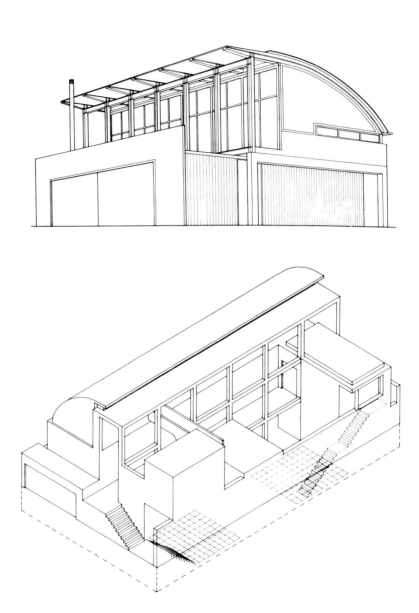

RICK MATHER ARCHITECTS

Zennw3, restaurant, London, 1986
Detail of staircase with water cascade
View towards entrance

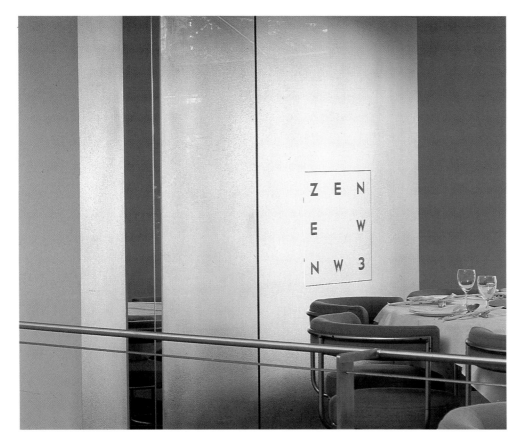

Zen Central, restaurant, London, 1987
Bar counter detail

Our initial design considerations are usually a balance of three things: what is appropriate to the surroundings, what will secure the most generous spaces inside, and what is the general type that satisfies the brief most effectively.

When building in an urban structure, our aim is to reinforce and develop a city that is convenient and pleasant for walking as well as driving, by maintaining the density of the city and reinforcing defined outdoor spaces.

Our aim with individual buildings is to make the most of the universal pleasures of natural light and sunshine. We like to bring natural light deep into the building and to build rooms with views that are varied, generous and well proportioned. The plan and section are basic to the design process. They are extensively worked and reworked to develop a route that will reveal, make sense of and connect the whole building. We try to make something of every element and component in the building so that they add to the richness of the design. Technology and energy conservation are important elements in the process but they are never the primary generators of a design.

Our aim in detailing and construction is to achieve an aesthetic where only the essential minimum is apparent. Our intention is to avoid modish and applied decoration that quickly ages. We try to achieve a lasting interest by using complex forms and sections with plain surfaces contrasting them with materials such as steel, glass, marble or wood. Plants are used as a counterpoint to the regularity of the building. In the composition of facades we aim to bring the complexity of the inside to the surface of the building to express clearly and legibly the internal organization of the building; and by bringing formality to outdoor space we try to create outdoor rooms which like their indoor counterparts are varied, generous and well proportioned.

We believe that any serious architect has an interest in and knowledge of the present and the past. Le Corbusier is a major reference because through his numerous publications he has most completely documented the preoccupations and language of the Modern Movement. But there are many favourites and influences (not to mention local friends as well): Unwin's and Rasmussen's attitude towards the city, Camillo Sitte's analysis of urban space; Soane's and Barry Parker's cross sections and large rooms; Corbusier's, Frank Lloyd Wright's and Mies Van der Rohe's (in his Barcelona period) routes and plan organization: Giulio Romano's and Lubetkin's facades: Palladio's and Craig Elwood's grids; Niemeyer's curves; Colin Rowe's way of looking at architectural history, etc.

Zen Restaurants

The owners of the Chinese restaurant ZEN in Chelsea commissioned these two works with the brief to produce an architecture for social dining that is as simple and elegant as their admired cuisine. The restaurants, occupying premises that were formally a lacklustre health restaurant and Post Office respectively, aim to strip away the ethnic culture of the type by concentrating on elemental qualities. Substantial rooflights were cut to illuminate the deep plans. Glass and water are used to exaggerate spatial velocity, water features being taken down the stair at Hampstead and down the entire length of the side wall at Mayfair.

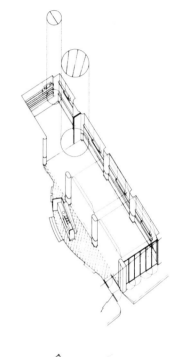

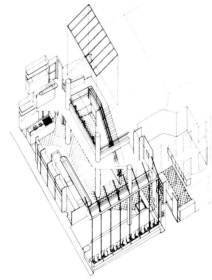

School of Education, Climatic Research building
University of East Anglia, Norwich, 1985

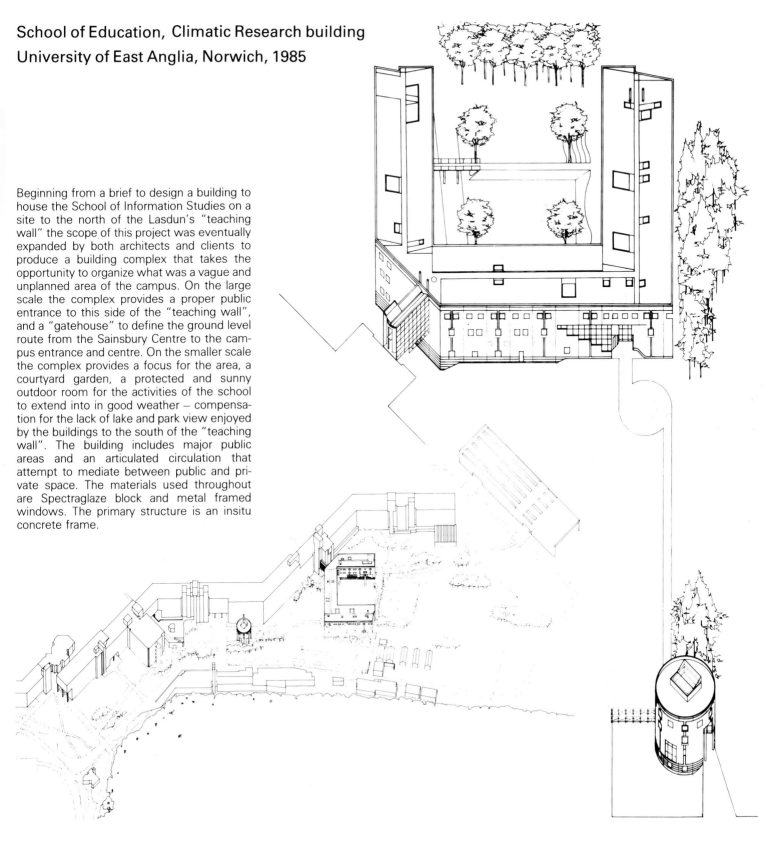

Beginning from a brief to design a building to house the School of Information Studies on a site to the north of the Lasdun's "teaching wall" the scope of this project was eventually expanded by both architects and clients to produce a building complex that takes the opportunity to organize what was a vague and unplanned area of the campus. On the large scale the complex provides a proper public entrance to this side of the "teaching wall", and a "gatehouse" to define the ground level route from the Sainsbury Centre to the campus entrance and centre. On the smaller scale the complex provides a focus for the area, a courtyard garden, a protected and sunny outdoor room for the activities of the school to extend into in good weather – compensation for the lack of lake and park view enjoyed by the buildings to the south of the "teaching wall". The building includes major public areas and an articulated circulation that attempt to mediate between public and private space. The materials used throughout are Spectraglaze block and metal framed windows. The primary structure is an insitu concrete frame.

Entrance facade

Entrance hall looking north

View of entrance hall

View of north-east corner of courtyard

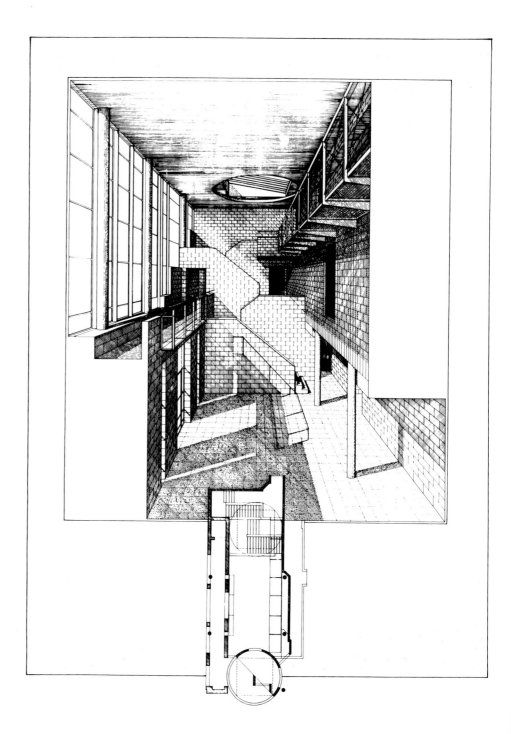

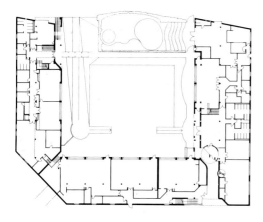

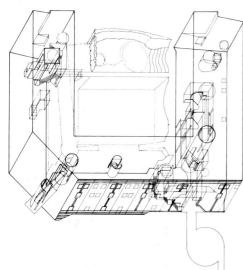

Ground floor plan

Axonometric

Perspective sketch of entrance hall

View from the west

Basement, ground, first and second floor plans

Exploded axonometric

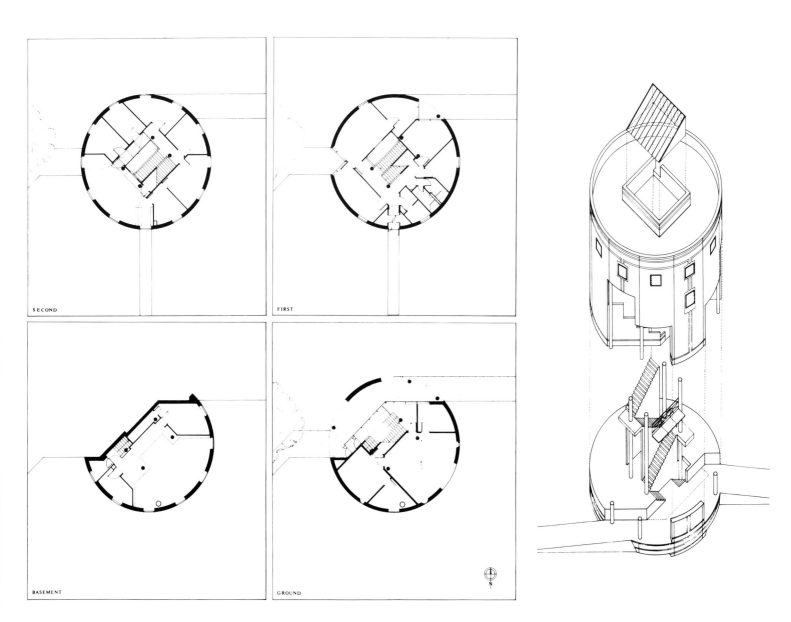

SECOND

FIRST

BASEMENT

GROUND

Penthouse, Point West, London, 1987

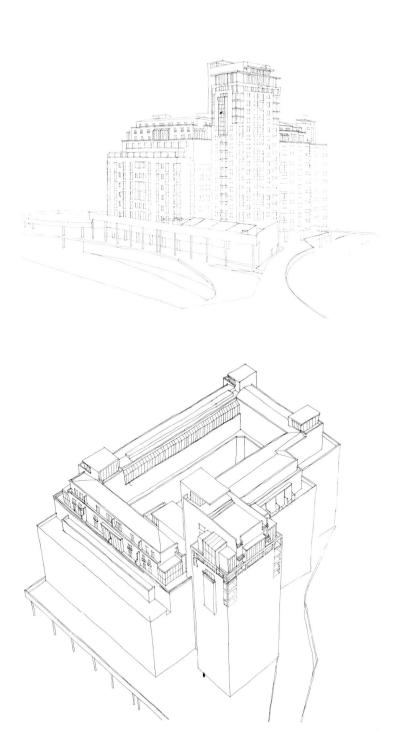

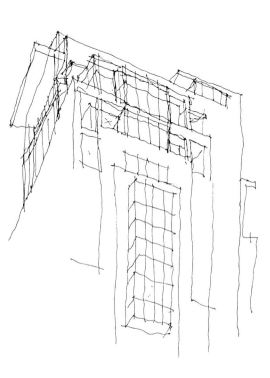

This triplex tops the new eighteen storey tower of the Point West development for whose key portions Rick Mather Architects are acting as consultants. The penthouse accommodation includes a double height conservatory, an indoor swimming pool, and a large roof garden. Externally, the form steps back to reveal the frame and major internal volumes to orientate the interior to the sun and spectacular views across the city and to make an interesting termination to the top of the building.

ERIC PARRY ASSOCIATES
14 Greek Street, London, 1987

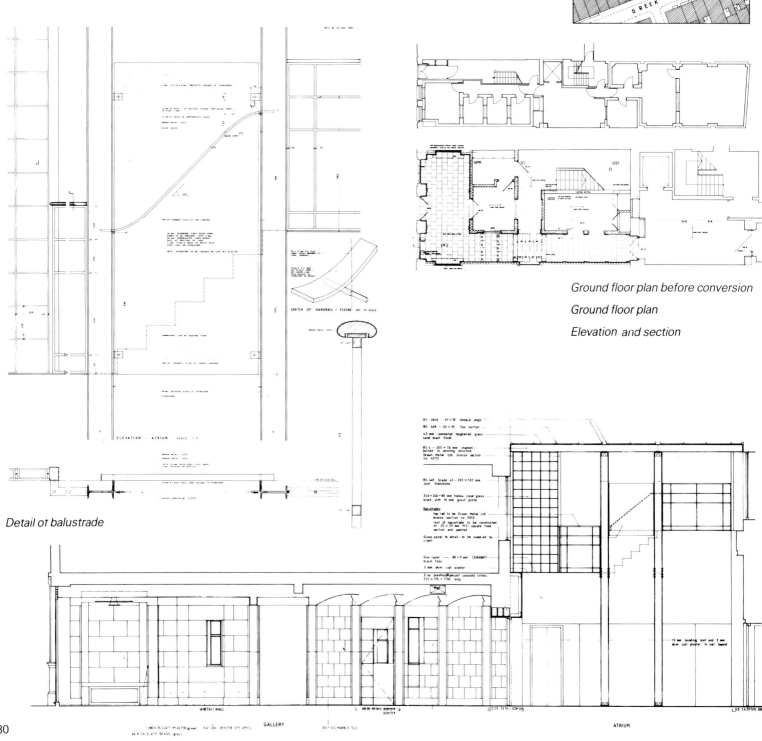

Detail ot balustrade

Ground floor plan before conversion

Ground floor plan

Elevation and section

GALLERY

ATRIUM

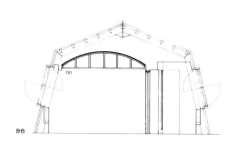

B-B

A-A

Third floor plan and sections

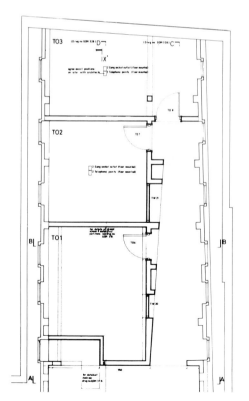

"I seek new perfumes, larger blossoms, pleasures still untasted."
Gustave Flaubert

Our clients, graphic designers and film animators, whose work is related to both the privacy and personal experience and the universality of mass media, together with a brief to refurbish an existing building in the heart of Soho (one of the most urban and public areas of London) gave rise to the spatial and material solution we sought: essentially, to mediate between the street and the interiority of the film studio.

The history of No 14 is typical of buildings in this area of London. Originally a 17th century terraced house with a courtyard on a deep plot, it was entirely rebuilt at the beginning of the century with the addition of a rear block separated from the original building by a lightwell. In the 1970's the site was refurbished for office use and was used more recently as a broadcasting school. The building as we found it precluded any contact with the street; a sound booth occupying two of the three facade bays. A solid front door gave access to a gloomy passage which passed under the landing of the listed stair, the only element remaining intact of the 17th century building.

We proposed as a response to the street and the symmetry of the facade the creation of an entrance space conceived as a loggia and as a consequence the materials and detail are sparse. This space acts as a transition between the street, the reception, seen as a casket with purpose made joinery, and the gallery through which the slate floor surface continues.

In the gallery we used the same materials articulated by the detail of openings, recesses and the introduction of more deliberate compositional devices. The lighting likewise is transformed from natural light with one central pendant fitting in the entrance to the continuous artificially lit vaults integral with the rhythm and proportions of the pilastered bays of the gallery. The gallery connects the loggia with the double height central space, which is conceived as an interior *cour d'honneur* containing a second tripartite facade of the building under a lay light. This facade faces a monumental wall to be articulated by a collage of fragments – a metaphorical study of the world within the building. Behind this *Scenae Frons* pass the occupants of the building. The articulation of the facade is achieved by the position of the universal columns relative to the landings and the steps. The balustrade becomes at the landings a virtual balcony overlooking the space, and the bronze handrails and screen frames echo the frames to the street.

Tom Phillips, from 'Dante's Inferno', 1985

Villa of the Physicist
External view

View of model of Tom Phillips' studio

Model by Nello Gregori

Artists studios, London, 1987

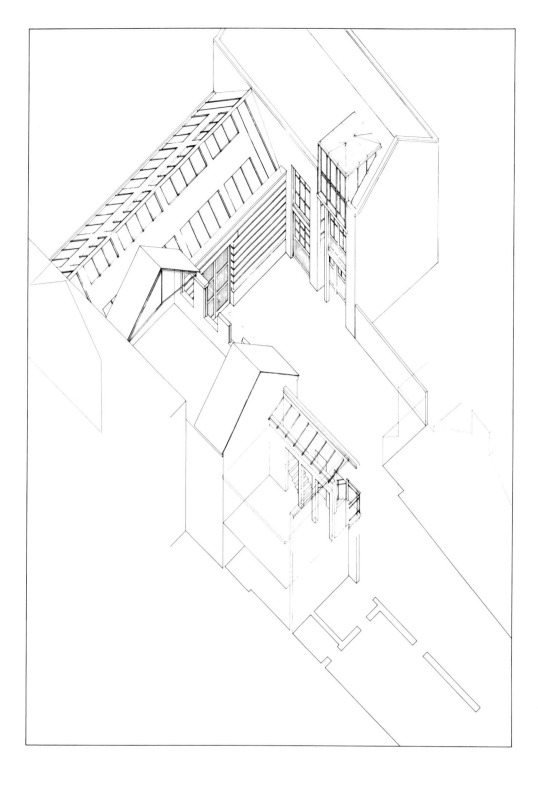

'Do you know what a painter's studio is like. . . it is a world in itself; a universe apart resembling our world in nothing.'
Theophile Gautier

The reality of the artist's studio often differs little from an uncomfortable workshop, yet it is also a place of reverie as Gautier suggests; as a result the studio brief clearly touches the core of any successful architecture, the alchemic combination of the prosaic and the poetic. As a reminder of the latter it is of course the place where bare matter is transformed at best into a work of art.

The studio has become for modern architecture the paradigmatic vision of dwelling; its allusions to individual creativity and freedom have been endlessly quoted in private houses and mass housing schemes alike, and so it was with understandable interest that we approached this opportunity to explore the problem of the work places of a painter and a sculptor.

The courtyard site, once a laundry and latterly a garage, is entered from Bellenden Road in South London through a gap in the terrace of shops. It consisted of the two primary buildings that have been retained (A and C) with a series of lean-to structures that have been demolished. Building C was purchased on behalf of the painter Tom Phillips by an American collector, whilst the remaining buildings are for the sculptor Antony Gormley. Both artists live near the site and it was this rather than a shared ideological position that drew them together.

The courtyard has been re-established with five principal elements: the rusticated brick wall, with its monumental door to Antony Gormley's sculpture studio (B); the tower of doors and windows to Tom Phillips' studio (C); the re-established elevation to building A; the stair and colonnade to building D; the fifth, unbuilt element, will be a canopy and gates at the entrance to the site.

Antony Gormley required one large space as his main studio (B) which could also be used to exhibit his work. This space was conceived as a neutral setting, determined by the clarity of his work and the landscapes and urban settings in which he places them. Top light is used to wash the walls, gable-ends and the central area of the long axis. Portal frames have been used to achieve an uninterrupted volume, with the frames set flush with the brick walls, as is the soffit of the ceiling, thus recessing the rooflights in the depth of the section.

The party wall created by the height of the sculpture studio between buildings B and C precluded any openings and the internalized space on the first floor of building C has become Tom Phillips' main painting studio lit by large north facing windows.

At the west end of this building a vertical section has been introduced which at ground level includes an entrance and exhibition space leading up to the entrance to the painting studio with a reading space under a mezzanine, which will also act as a smaller studio and gallery to the main space. The principal stair wraps around a *columna memorialis* which will house a collection of books and objects, as will cabinets that form screens between the reading space and the studio. Beyond the ground floor exhibiton space is a printing and etching studio lit by roof lights.

Externally the stair column is echoed in a concrete column that creates a double height niche, suggesting a scale greater than the domestic. The entrance doors are supressed in the depth of the facade, allowing paintings to be lowered to the courtyard from a slotted trap door at the first floor. The mezzanine created as a gallery to the painting studio becomes externally a belvedere, the windows to which are also supressed behind the steel dormer structure.

Building A is at ground floor a workshop for materials with hand and power tools, at first floor level a painting and drawing studio reached by the external steel stair and top-lit colonnade. The elevations to the courtyard are designed to create an order to this urban interior, to evoke, as Bachelard describes in his *Poetics of Space*, a state of intimate immensity.

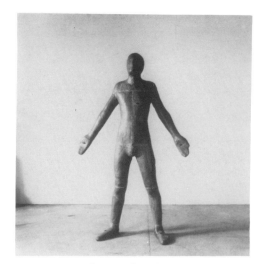

Antony Gormley 'Untitled', 1985

Section looking north

Section looking west

Section looking south.

Ground floor plan

LOCATION PLAN

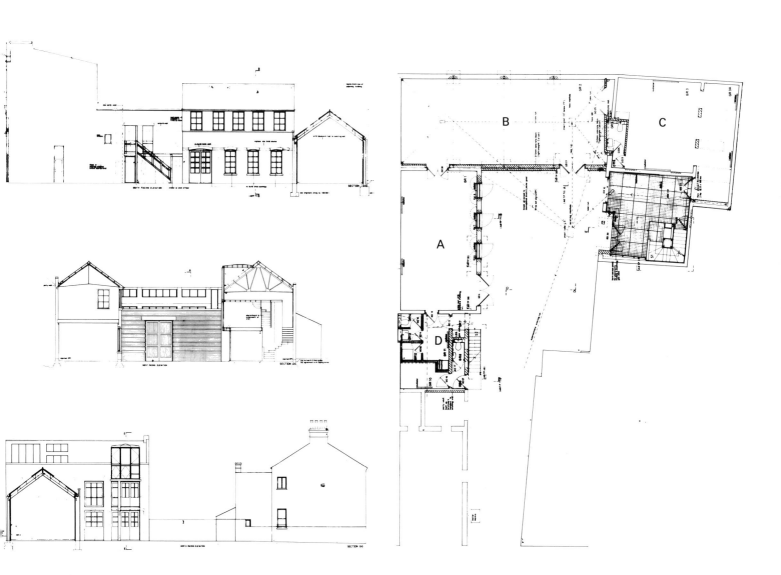

Villa of the Physicists

"The climate is murderous but the air conditioning is excellent."
Friedrich Durrenmatt

The situation for which this villa is a setting is derived from Friedrich Durrenmatt's play *'The Physicists'*. Durrenmatt describes the landscape in which he envisages the villa as being *'in a superficial way restful to the nerves; there are blue mountain ranges, hills geometrically afforested and a fairly large lake, as well as a broad plain, once a dismal moor, which turns misty in the evenings and is crisscrossed by canals and irrigation ditches and is therefore very fertile.'*

In the play the villa is inhabited by three protagonists and their attendants. The villa was not designed specifically for these people nor was it intended for the use to which it has been put, an asylum. This interpretation is only an extreme vision of the tradition of the European villa, which is one of removal but dependence on urbanity. I have interpreted this tradition of the villa in a contemporary context adhering to Durrenmatt's view that as the action takes place amongs madmen it *'therefore requires a classical framework to keep it in shape'*. This apparent unity is one formed and dependent on the combination of opposites; country/city, nature/artifice, earth/sky. The play likewise is constructed around several oppositions; outside/inside, sane/insane, villa/asylum, care/murder and it is through these that the levels of removal of the villa can be interpreted.

Woven through the main drama are several activities which provide mediating experiences between the realm of the theoretical investigation of the physicists and the murder investigation of the Inspector. There are varying levels of abstraction, writing, music, chess, dining and conversation. The organization of the villa reflects the hierarchy taking as a point of departure for the interpretation of oppositions the centrally planned temple/pavilion form of villa.

From the point of view of the inhabitants, the villa is the white stucco interior that one would expect, whilst from the outside the temple/pavilion becomes a black mausoleum. This inverse play on themes, like the light of understanding is meant to correspond to Mobius' central perception (Act II) *'we know a few precisely-calculable laws, a few basic connexions between incomprehensible phenomena, and that is all. The rest is mystery closed to the rational mind . . . for as physicists there is nothing left but to surrender to reality . . . either we stay in this madhouse or the world becomes one.'*

Basement plan

Ground floor plan

First floor plan

Second floor plan

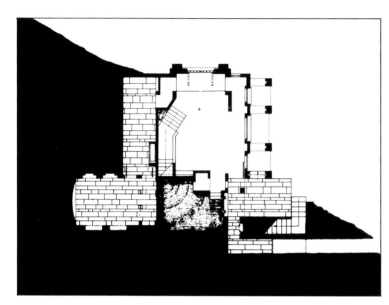

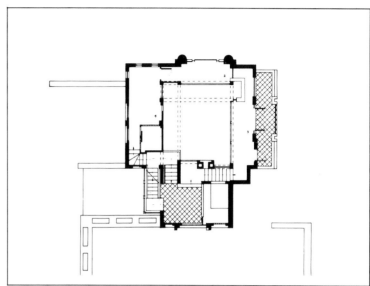

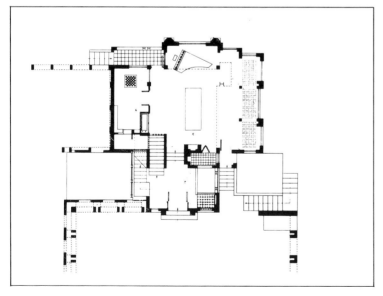

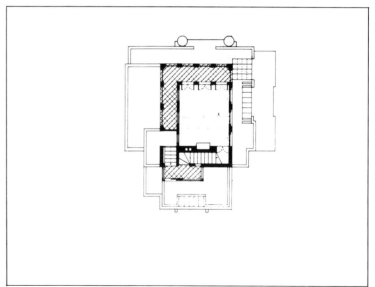

37

We are exhibiting three projects, one complete, one under construction and the third unbuilt. The built projects are represented by drawings, models and photographs that illustrate the spatial and material development of the schemes. The theoretical project is represented by drawings that illustrate different aspects of one particular stage in its evolution. Together they form a typical cross section of the work and working methods currently adopted.

As a practice we consider ourselves to be part of a wider group of architects concerned with the bridge between theory and practice, who have been influenced by the teaching of Dalibor Vesely and Peter Carl. Vesely's profound interpretation of the nature of architectural space has been particularly important in the development of our own approach, which is based principally on an interest in the contemporary city. It is in the city that the most complete embodiment of contemporary culture is to be found; and it is only by direct or indirect reference to the city that we find it possible to judge the plausibility of a *parti* and appropriateness of the detail as a manifestation of the whole.

STANTON WILLIAMS

Tate Gallery Pavilions, (Alan Stanton and Peter Rice)

Rodin Exhibition, Hayward Gallery, 1986

Currently, many of our projects are concerned with art exhibitions and gallery design. A conscious style is avoided in the belief that each project is unique and demands its own approach and solutions. Aware of the intimate relationship between viewer, object and space, it is our fundamental aim to develop a way of designing that brings together, integrates and unifies these elements. Exhibitions offer a variety of problems and objectives with relatively short periods of realization and therefore offer us a platform to experiment with both subtle changes in emphasis and basic forms of interpretation.

There are many constraints in designing with art objects. Curatorial requirements – the selection and grouping of objects, and often the sheer number of objects that must be shown – may oppose aesthetic priorities. Conservation requirements: environmental temperature and humidity control, alarm systems and protective glass specifications can intervene between object and viewer. Low levels of lighting can often be at variance with the desired lighting for the architectural space. Solutions must be sought that reveal the intellectual and historical content of an object while giving full value to its visual impact.

Most recent museum architecture seems to be conceived either in the tradition of 18th or 19th century galleries, or as an abstract container. The design of many museums stops far short of the proper consideration of the objects they display. It is all too easy to articulate the architectural space by furnishing it with objects. Conversely, many object displays and interiors fail to relate to the architecture of existing galleries. It was a typical approach in the 1960s and 1970s to suppress original spaces by the introduction of false walls and ceilings simply in order to focus on the display. Although we sympathize with current attitudes that favour restoration of the architecture, the spaces created often have nothing in common with the objects being shown, both in scale and detail. It is the

area that recognizes both the needs of the object and the overall space that we now find ourselves exploring. A successful gallery should liberate the forces of an object and, by careful selection and placing of the objects, move people through spaces that naturally form part of the overall architecture.

Our aim is to design coherent spaces by clearly structuring horizontal and vertical planes, introducing repeated elements where necessary that set up rhythms to move the eye through the space and focus down onto objects. Weight and emphasis are achieved with colour and light, the latter being used to define the architectural space, model forms and reveal details.

Ultimately, we hope to achieve a balance of components that allows the viewer to develop his own individual interpretation – something that is potentially greater than the sum of the parts.

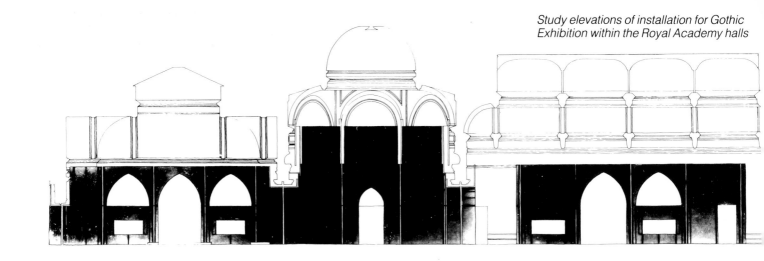

The exhibition demonstrates the visual splendour, the craftsmanship and the powerful imagery of Gothic art. There are brilliantly coloured stained glass windows and tiny precious jewels, sumptuous embroideries and illuminated manuscripts, paintings and intricate metalwork, large sculptures of wood and stone and intimate carved ivories, misericords, pottery, coins and seals. Architecture is shown in especially commissioned photographs and in an audio visual display.

The exhibition takes the visitor chronologically through the reigns of the five Plantangenet Kings, showing the relationship between the different media, the importance of patronage, and the development of the Gothic style. Interposed within the historical arrangement will be four galleries devoted to the themes of royalty, pilgrimage, the social hierarchy and the techniques of medieval art.

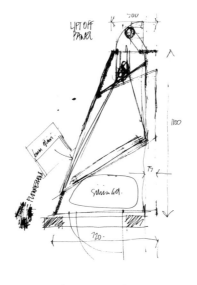

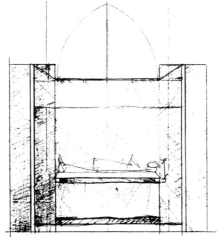

Prototype of timber arch for exhibition installation

Detail of showcase and exhibition stand

Romaneque Exhibition: the bare structure during installation at the Hayward Gallery

Romanesque Exhibition: the environment is transformed by lighting and the presence of the exhibited objects

Two statues destined for the Romanesque Exhibition in situ

The statues displayed at the Romanesque Exhibition, Hayward Gallery

Miyake Man, Fulham Road, London, 1987
Issey Miyake collection

Given the context (a narrow four storey shop building) we responded to Miyake's subtle fabrics and strong forms by building a dramatic space with rich but simple materials. Two floors were removed from the original building and walls and ceilings rendered in Italian Marmorina plaster. A wide stone stair moves downwards from the entrance to the alcoves where the clothes are displayed. Entrance doors and furniture are in English oak.

At the rear of the shop, a rooflight brings daylight vertically down through the volume. Other (artificial) lighting is hidden or recessed in ceiling or wall cavities.

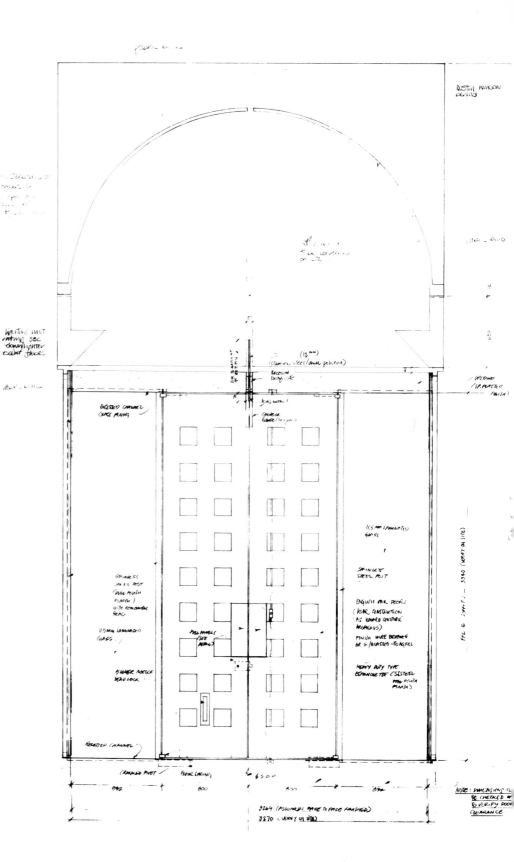

Section of gallery balustrade

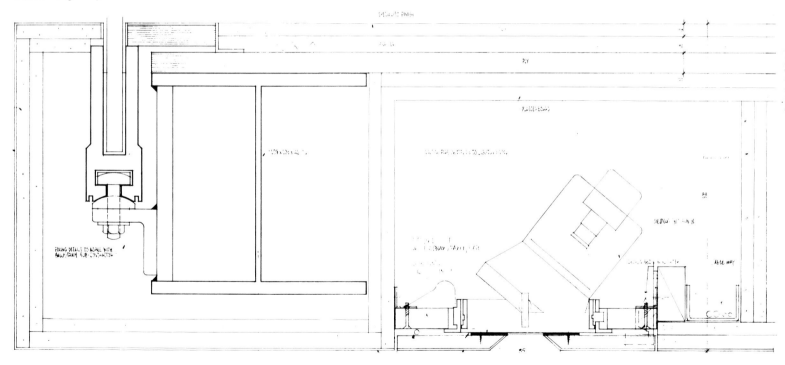

Miyake Man, Fulham Road, London, 1987

View from the entrance showing vaulted ceiling and cantilevered floor at ground level

Miyake Man, view from the basement area towards the entrance door in english oak

The RIBA Gallery, Portland Place, London, 1987
(winning competition entry)

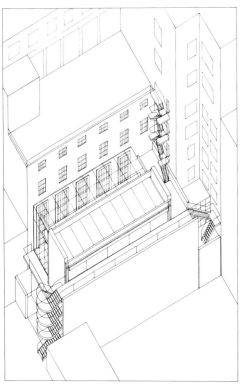

Stanton Williams won the competition for a new gallery for the RIBA headquarters building in Portland Place in January 1987. The design provides a flexible, high quality gallery space, that complements the Florence Hall and its windows.

The concept for the gallery is based upon a (potentially) closed inner 'box' with controlled light and microclimate. Surrounding this is an open space that forms a 'galleria' along the Florence Hall windows and provides foyer and access areas.

The external delivery/fire escape route is placed at roof level to allow adequate space for: a 'galleria' that maintains daylighting, views and scale appropriate to the Florence Hall windows; a flexible exhibition area with the potential of movement both across and along the space – necessary for the well structured presentation of drawings.

There are no important views to the rear of the gallery, but the 'galleria' end window allows a view of the mews for orientation and reference. The proposed line of rooflight 'frames' the Florence Hall windows and improves the proportions of the facade.

The gallery space is multi-purpose; it may be used in conjunction with the Florence Hall; as a low light-level display space; for small or large exhibitions; as an open space, maintaining the feeling of the existing courtyard.

Location of proposed RIBA Gallery over the existing sculpture court, Portland Place London

Alternative operating layouts: open;
controlled environment; exhibition
preparation

View from foyer

Cross section

Plan

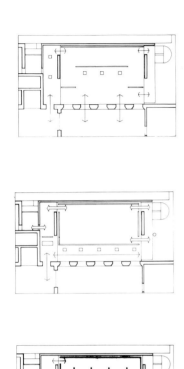

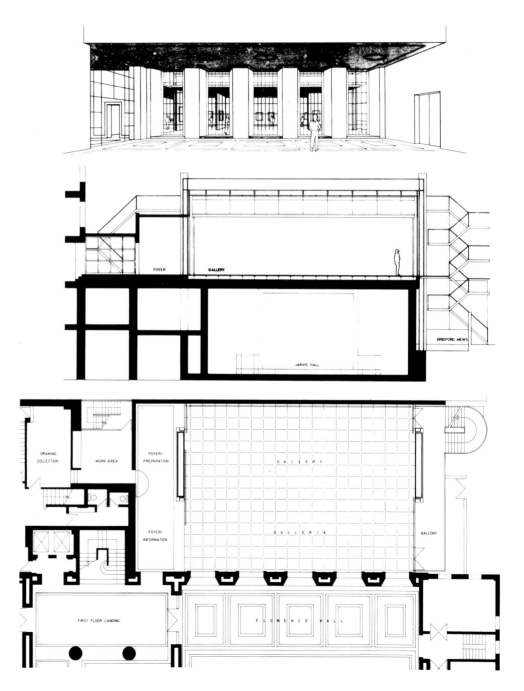

Stanton & Williams: Japan Gallery, Victoria and Albert Museum, 1986

Katsura palace, Japan

The brief presented the problem of showing a large number of small Japanese artefacts in a Victorian gallery at the Victoria and Albert Museum with a very high ceiling. In accordance with the Museum's policy of respect for its existing architecture, the disparity in size and aesthetic has been resolved by the creation of a setting at ground level which does not obstruct the Victorian vista.

The materials suggest the traditional Japanese interior without direct imitation. The dark satin finish of the timbers in Japanese houses is echoed in the stained iroko wood of the display structure. This incorporates light-coloured walls framed in wood, and interlocking forms including panels of closely-set vertical members.

Traditional arrangements of art objects stress the harmonious grouping of diverse materials on a single plane. The museum convention of 'blocks' which artificially alter relative heights is therefore avoided. In the same way that Japanese interior architecture it typified by the adaptability of spaces, objects can be substituted or rearranged at will in each of the two types of showcase in the gallery.

CHIPPERFIELD ASSOCIATES

The practice was founded in October 1984 by David Chipperfield (born 1953) on leaving Foster Associates. Over the last two years the work completed includes shops, offices, residential interiors, private houses and furniture. Current projects include private museums in Boston and Tokyo, the remodelling of the Arnolfini Gallery in Bristol and various residential developments in London. The practice is currently working in association with Skidmore, Owings and Merrill, Frank Gehry and Jacqueline Robertson on several urban planning projects in London.

David Chipperfield trained at the Architectural Association and worked for some major architectural practices including Richard Rogers and Foster Associates. He is a director of the 9H Gallery and most recently he was a visiting professor in Architecture at Harvard.

The work has been published extensively in England, France, Japan and the USA. An exhibition of furniture will be held in Tokyo in the Autumn.

Practice members:
David Chipperfield, John Southall, Robert Maxwell, Simon Colebrook, Aubrey Newman, Michael Greville, Janelle Plummer, Jonathan Sergison, Andrew Bryce, Amanda Callaghan

RICK MATHER ARCHITECTS

Rick Mather (born 1937) studied architecture in the United States and Urban Design at the Architectural Association. He taught at the Architectural Association, Bartlett School and Polytechnic of Central London and worked in various offices in the United States and London before setting up his own office in 1972. The office currently numbers 10 architectural and two support staff.

Practice members:
Rick Mather, Elena Acciarri, Robert Brennan, Jim Conti, Tom Croft, Charles Emberson, Edward Finnamore, Mark Guard, Bill Greensmith, Mark Gregg, Ian Hay, Steve Keyser, Pascal Madoc-Jones, Dan Naegele, David Naessous, Antoinette O'Neill, Carolyn Trevor, Brian O'Tuama, Thomas Young

ERIC PARRY ASSOCIATES

The practice was formed in 1985 by Eric Parry (born 1952) who has been a lecturer at the Department of Architecture, Cambridge University, since 1982. Parry has worked in association with Doug Clelland on the Solid State building (1979-81) in Oxfordshire and more recently on a number of projects with Dalibor Veseley. The practice is engaged in a number of conversions of existing buildings in London and an extension to a Chateau in France.

Practice members:
Eric Parry, Christopher Wong, Nello Gregori, Michael Mallinson

STANTON WILLIAMS

The practice was established in 1986 as a collaboration between Alan Stanton (born 1944) and Paul Williams (born 1947). Stanton worked Piano and Rogers on the Centres Georges Pompidou in Paris and together with Mike Dowd recently completed the major exhibition space at the Museum of Science and Industry, La Villette, Paris. Paul Williams was trained in three-dimensional design and has been responsible for a number of major exhibitions at the Hayward Gallery (English Romanesque Art; Matisse) and other institutions in the UK. Together, Stanton Williams have won the competition for a new gallery at the RIBA in London (1987), and are currently working on numerous museum and exhibition projects.

Practice members:
Alan Stanton, Paul Williams, William Firebrace, Geraldine Flashman, Russel Gilchrist, David Gomersall, Georgina Hamilton-Fletcher, Tony O'Neill, Wendy Robin, Marianne Ryan, John Wilson.